PASTA
cookbook

BRIDGET JONES

A QUINTET BOOK

ISBN: 0–7858–0493–5

This book was designed and produced by
Quintet Publishing Limited

Creative Director: Richard Dewing
Designer: Ian Hunt
Project Editor: Katie Preston
Editor: Diana Vowles
Photographer: Trevor Wood
Illustrator: Annie Ellis
Jacket Design: Nik Morley

Typeset in Great Britain by
Central Southern Typesetters, Eastbourne

Produced in Australia by Griffin Colour

Published by Chartwell Books
A Division of Book Sales, Inc.
P.O. Box 7100
Edison, New Jersey 08818–7100

Contents

1 PASTA PERFECT EVERY TIME 4

    Equipment   4

    Pasta Making Techniques   5

    Pasta Dough   9

2 PASTA SIMPLE IN ITS PRIME 11

3 DRESSINGS AND SAUCES FOR FRESH PASTA . . . 15

4 HOT CREATIONS: Timbales, Molds and Bakes . . . 27

5 STUFFED PASTA: Fillings for Flavor 29

6 PASTA COOL: The Freshest Salad Ideas 34

7 PASTA INTERNATIONAL: Doughs from around the World   40

8 PASTA FOR DESSERT: Sweet Dishes to Delight . . . 46

EQUIPMENT

You do not need any·special equipment for making pasta. A large area of work surface helps, but it is not essential as you can always roll the dough in two or more batches. A mixing bowl, spoon and rolling pin are the basics, and an extra-long rolling pin is useful (make sure an ordinary one does not have knobs at the ends as they indent the dough and make rolling out difficult). You may also wish to invest in some of the following:

Pastry Wheel A fluted pastry wheel for cutting out ravioli.

Ravioli Tray A small metal tray with round or square hollows. Lay a sheet of pasta over the tray, press it in neatly and spoon mixture into the hollows. Brush with egg, cover with a second sheet of dough and roll the top to seal before cutting out the ravioli.

Pasta Machine A small but heavy metal machine for rolling pasta. Fitted with plain rollers which can be set at different distances apart, this basic, inexpensive machine is terrific. Once the dough is briefly kneaded, rolling it through the machine several times on the widest setting will complete the kneading.

Set the rollers at the narrow width for rolling out sheets of dough or substitute cutting rollers to make noodles or spaghetti. A ravioli filler attachment makes very small, neat ravioli by feeding the pasta and filling through a hopper-like attachment.

Electric Pasta Machines Large, expensive machines are available for mixing, kneading, rolling and extruding pasta. Unless you are an avid pasta eater, this is an unlikely piece of equipment for the average domestic kitchen.

Pasta Dryer A small wooden rack on which to hang cut noodles or sheets of pasta as they are rolled out.

BELOW
Hand-turned pasta machine with attachments for filled pasta.

PASTA-MAKING TECHNIQUES

Mixing and Kneading

Unlike pastry, pasta dough needs a firm hand and a positive approach to mixing and kneading. The dough will seem very dry and prone to crumbling at first but as you knead it, the oil and egg combine fully with the flour and the ingredients bind together.

1 Mix the ingredients in the bowl, using a spoon at first, then your hand.

2 Begin the kneading process in the bowl, bringing the dough together and "wiping" the bowl clean of any crumbs.

3 Turn the dough out on to a lightly floured, clean surface and knead it into a ball. Add a little flour to the work surface to prevent the dough sticking, but try to keep this to the minimum during kneading.

4 Once the dough has come together, knead it firmly and rhythmically, pressing it down and out in one movement, then pulling the edge of the dough back in towards the middle in the next movement. Keep turning the dough as you knead it, so that you work it around in a circle rather than constantly pressing and pulling one side. Keep the dough moving and it will not stick to the surface.

5 The dough is ready when it is smooth and warm. Wrap it in a polythene bag or cling film and set it aside for 15–30 minutes if possible before rolling it out.

Rolling Out

When rolling the dough, try to keep it in the shape you want to end up with. Press the dough flat, forming it into an oblong or square, then roll it out firmly. Lift and "shake out" the dough a few times initially to ensure it does not stick to the surface. As the dough becomes thinner you have to handle it more carefully to avoid splitting it. However, pasta dough is far more durable than pastry and the smoother it becomes as it is rolled, the tougher it is. It can be rolled out very thinly – until you can almost see through it – without breaking, but this is not essential for the majority of pasta dishes. Dust the surface under the dough with a little flour occasionally, as necessary, and dust the top, rubbing the flour over the dough with one hand. Continue rolling until the dough is thin and even – a common mistake is to leave the dough too thick, so that it becomes unpleasantly solid when cooked. For noodles, or pasta which is to be eaten plain or topped with sauce, try to roll out to the thickness of a piece of brown paper: this makes excellent noodles.

Make sure the surface under the dough is sifted with flour, then cover the dough completely with cling film and leave for 10 minutes. This relaxes the dough before cutting – it is not essential but does prevent the dough from shrinking as it is cut.

ABOVE
Fruit and vegetable stall in Pienza, Italy.

Cutting Pasta

You need a large, sharp knife and a large floured platter or tray on which to place the pasta (a clean roasting tin will do). Flour the dough lightly before cutting. Once cut, keep the pasta dusted with flour to prevent it sticking together. Pasta may be dried before cooking by hanging it on a rack or spreading it out. I have, before now, draped pasta between two chair backs (covering them with kitchen paper first). Quite honestly, I have not found any great advantage to drying the pasta and have always felt that it is thoroughly inconvenient and unhygienic. It seems to cook well if it is added to boiling water straight after rolling.

Sheets Trim the dough edges so that they are straight, then cut the pasta into squares or oblongs. This is basic lasagne, so cut the dough to suit the size of dish.

Noodles Dust the dough well with flour, then roll it up. Use a sharp knife to cut the roll into 5 mm/¼ in wide slices. Shake out the slices as they are cut and they fall into long noodles. Keep the noodles floured and loosely piled on the tray to prevent them from sticking together. Cover loosely with cling film.

Circles or shapes Use biscuit cutters and aspic cutters to stamp out circles and shapes.

Squares Trim the dough edges, then use a clean, long ruler to cut the dough into wide strips. Cut these across into squares.

Small squares Use a ruler to cut the dough into 2.5 cm/1 in wide strips, then cut these across into squares. The small squares may be cooked and treated as bought pasta shapes.

Other shapes If you have the time, you can make other shapes by hand. Cut the dough into strips, then into small oblongs or squares. By twisting, pleating or pinching you can make bows and funny little twists and, I am sure, lots of clever alternatives. Frankly, I feel inclined to leave this to the manufacturers as it is very time-consuming.

Ravioli

Cut the pasta dough in half. Roll out one half into an oblong measuring slightly larger than 35.5 × 25 cm/14 × 10 in. Trim the edges of the dough neatly. Cover the rolled out dough with cling film, then roll out the second portion of dough in the same way but do not bother to trim the edges this time, as a little more dough is needed to cover the stuffing.

Dot small balls of the meat mixture in even lines over the neat oblong of pasta dough, leaving a gap of about 2 cm/¾ in between them. You should have 34–36 ravioli. Whisk a little water into the remaining beaten egg, to make it go further if necessary, then brush it over the dough between the mounds of meat. Carefully lay the second sheet of dough over the top. Starting at one end, seal the dough around the meat, carefully pressing out the air and flattening the meat slightly to seal the packages. Use a sharp knife or pastry wheel to trim the pasta edges and cut between the mounds of meat. Make sure the ravioli are neat and flour them slightly, if necessary, to prevent them sticking together.

LEFT
Home-made fresh pasta squares.

RIGHT
Home-made fresh pasta bows.

Cooking Fresh Pasta

Pasta should be cooked in enormous quantities of boiling water. Although you can get away with less water than the volume which is always suggested for authentic recipes (which means using a stock pot or catering-size pan when cooking enough for four people), you need a large saucepan which holds 3.4–3.9 litres/6–7 pt to cook 350–450 g/12–16 oz pasta. If you have a stock pot or very large pressure cooker which you can use without the lid on, so much the better.

Pour water into the pan to three-quarters of its capacity. Add salt and bring the water to the boil. Adding a little oil to the water helps to prevent it from frothing on the surface and boiling over rapidly – the pasta will not stick together if you have a pan which is large enough, and adding oil does little to prevent the pasta sticking in a pan which is too small! Add the pasta when the water is fully boiling, give it a stir and bring the water back to the boil rapidly. Be ready to reduce the heat otherwise the water will froth over. Cook for about 3 minutes for noodles and other types of unfilled pasta. Filled pasta requires longer to allow the filling to cook through.

When cooked, the pasta should be "al dente" (with bite). It should be firm yet tender, not soft or sticky. Drain the cooked pasta at once, pouring it into a large colander. Shake the colander over the sink, then tip the pasta into a hot bowl and add the dressing or sauce. Serve at once.

Chilling Prepared Pasta

Dust the pasta with plenty of flour and place it in a large airtight container in the refrigerator. Cook within 2 days of making or freeze promptly. The unrolled dough may be wrapped and chilled for 1–2 days.

Leftover Cooked Pasta

Cool quickly and chill in a covered container. Reheat pasta in the microwave or in a sauce on the hob or in the oven.

Freezing Pasta

Uncooked fresh pasta freezes very well but it is best to roll and cut the dough first. Separate sheets of pasta by interleaving freezer film between them. Flour noodles and pack them loosely in polythene bags, then spread them out fairly flat for freezing, so they do not form a lump. Bought fresh pasta is an excellent freezer candidate which is ideal for impromptu meals.

Do not thaw frozen pasta before cooking, simply add it to boiling water and cook as for fresh pasta. Noodles and most other shapes take about the same time to cook as unfrozen pasta, once the water has come to the boil again. Frozen filled pasta requires extra cooking time to allow the filling to thaw and cook properly.

Cooked lasagne and cannelloni or similar layered pasta dishes freeze well but cooked shapes and noodles tend to have an inferior texture if frozen after cooking.

USING THE RECIPES

☛ Use either metric or Imperial quantities, not a mixture of both as they are not interchangeable.

☛ All spoon measures refer to standard measuring spoons. Do not use table cutlery as the volume will vary. Quantities refer to level measuring spoons.

tbsp = tablespoon   tsp = teaspoon

☛ Oven temperatures refer to conventional ovens; if you have a forced convection oven, please refer to the manufacturer's instructions for adapting cooking times or temperatures.

☛ Unless otherwise stated, herbs are fresh, not dried.

☛ Eggs are size 3 unless otherwise stated.

RIGHT
Traditional Italian ham and wines at a restaurant in Monte Reggiano, Tuscany.

Pasta Dough

MAKES ABOUT 600 G/1¼ LB PASTA

350 g/12 oz strong plain flour
1 tsp salt
3 eggs
4 tbsp olive oil
1 tbsp water

Mix the flour and salt together in a large bowl. Make a well in the middle, then add the eggs, olive oil and water. Use a spoon to mix the eggs, oil and water, gradually working in the flour. When the mixture begins to bind into clumps, scrape the spoon clean and knead the dough together with your hands.

Press the dough into a ball and roll it around the bowl to leave the bowl completely clean of the mixture. Then turn the dough out on a lightly floured, clean surface and knead it thoroughly until it is smooth. Follow the notes on kneading, keeping the dough moving and adding the minimum extra flour required to prevent it sticking as you work. Wrap the dough in a polythene bag and leave it to rest for 15–30 minutes before rolling it out. Do not chill the dough as this will make it difficult to handle.

Mixing the dough.

Flavoured Pasta

The following may be used with the above recipe.

Beetroot Purée 50 g/2 oz cooked and peeled beetroot with 2 eggs in a food processor or liquidizer, or press it through a sieve (this eliminates dark speckles). Add the beetroot purée with the remaining egg. Omit the oil and water. Do not use beetroot which has been preserved in acetic acid or vinegar: it must be freshly boiled or the untreated vacuum-packed type.

Carrot Omit half the oil and water but add 2 tbsp carrot juice with the eggs. Natural carrot juice is available from wholefood shops and delicatessens.

Herb Add 4 tbsp chopped mixed fresh herbs to the flour and salt. Suitable herbs include parsley, thyme, sage, tarragon, chives, chervil, marjoram and fennel. Rosemary may be used but only in very small quantities as it is a strongly flavoured herb. Balance the delicate herbs against the stronger ones by using less of the latter. Use two, three or more herbs but remember that a delicate herb like dill will be totally lost if combined with many other herbs. Dill is best mixed with chives and a little parsley.

Olive Finely chop 100 g/4 oz black olives and add them to the flour.

Spinach Wash and trim 225 g/8 oz fresh spinach. Place the damp leaves in a saucepan. Cover tightly and cook over high heat for 5 minutes, shaking the pan often. Turn the spinach into a sieve placed over a basin. Press and squeeze all the juice from the spinach, leaving the leaves as dry as possible. Add 6 tbsp spinach juice to the pasta and omit the oil and water.

Tomato Add 1 tbsp concentrated tomato purée, beating it into the eggs.

Turmeric Add 1 tsp ground turmeric to the flour. For a pleasing, unusual, lightly spiced pasta, add 1 tbsp white cumin seeds to the flour with the turmeric.

Walnut Use walnut oil instead of olive oil.

Won Ton Dough

MAKES ABOUT 350 G/12 OZ DOUGH

175 g/6 oz plain flour
50 g/2 oz cornflour
pinch of salt
1 egg, beaten
100 ml/4 fl oz water

Sift the flour, cornflour and salt into a bowl, then make a well in the middle. Add the egg and pour in the water. Use a spoon to mix the egg and water into the flour. When the mixture binds together, scrape the spoon clean and use your hand to work the dough into a smooth ball, leaving the bowl free of mixture.

Turn the dough out on a clean surface and knead it thoroughly until it is very smooth. Cut the dough in half and wrap both portions in polythene or cling film, then set aside for 15–30 minutes.

Roll out one portion of dough at a time. Dust the work surface and rolling pin lightly with cornflour, then roll out the dough as required until it is thin and even.

When rolling out the dough for won tons, try to keep it in a square shape, then trim the edges. Use a clean, long ruler as a guide for cutting the dough in wide strips, then cut in the opposite direction to make squares.

Alternatively, a plain round biscuit cutter may be used to stamp rounds out of the dough for making various dim sum, such as dumplings and packets.

Pasta with Butter and Parmesan

SERVES 4

75 g/3 oz butter

75 g/3 oz freshly grated parmesan cheese

450 g/1 lb pasta

freshly ground black pepper

Soften the butter, then gradually mix in the parmesan cheese and beat the mixture until it is soft and creamy. Dot it over the drained pasta, then toss well and add freshly ground black pepper to taste. Serve at once.

Spaghetti with Walnuts and Olives

SERVES 4

75 ml/3 fl oz olive oil

knob of butter

1 garlic clove, crushed (optional)

175 g/6 oz walnuts, finely chopped

100 g/4 oz black olives, roughly chopped

2 tbsp capers, chopped

4 tbsp chopped parsley

freshly ground black pepper

450 g/1 lb spaghetti

Heat the oil and butter with the garlic (if using) until the butter melts. Stir in the walnuts, cook gently for 2 minutes, then add the olives, capers, parsley, a little salt and plenty of freshly ground black pepper. Pour the mixture over the drained spaghetti, toss well and serve at once.

BELOW
*The beautiful area called Crete,
south of Siena, Italy.*

Spirals with Grapes and Goat's Cheese

This is delicious for a light lunch or as a starter. Serve with slices of French bread.

SERVES 4

2 slices round chèvre goat's cheese, each cut in 8 small wedges
175 g/6 oz seedless green grapes
2 bunches of watercress, trimmed and roughly shredded
4 spring onions, chopped
grated rind and juice of 1 orange
4 tbsp olive oil
salt and freshly ground black pepper
350 g/12 oz pasta spirals

Mix the cheese, grapes, watercress and spring onions in a large bowl. Pour in the orange rind and juice and olive oil, then add a little salt and plenty of freshly ground black pepper. Mix well. Divide the hot, freshly drained pasta between four serving plates, then top each with a quarter of the cheese mixture. Serve at once.

Spaghetti with Smoked Sausage and Carrots

A good, inexpensive and satisfying supper dish: the sweetness of the carrot complements the flavoursome sausage. Try to find smoked sausage made with fresh garlic.

SERVES 4

3 tbsp olive oil
1 onion, halved and thinly sliced
225 g/8 oz carrots, coarsely grated
450 g/1 lb smoked sausage, cut into strips
salt and freshly ground black pepper
450 g/1 lb spaghetti
50 g/2 oz butter

Heat the oil in a large frying pan. Add the onion and cook for 5 minutes, then add the carrots and sausage. Cook, stirring often, for about 10 minutes, until the pieces of sausage are browned in parts and the carrots are lightly cooked. Add seasoning to taste. Add the butter to the carrot and sausage mixture, toss the lot into the drained spaghetti and serve at once.

13

Pasta with Mixed Mushrooms

SERVES 4

25 g/1 oz dried mushrooms
300 ml/½ pt dry white wine
50 g/2 oz butter
225 g/8 oz chestnut mushrooms, sliced
225 g/8 oz oyster mushrooms, sliced
300 ml/½ pt single cream
salt and freshly ground black pepper
3 tbsp chopped parsley
450 g/1 lb pasta
freshly grated parmesan cheese, to serve

Place the dried mushrooms in a basin and pour the wine over them. Cover with a saucer and weight it down to keep the mushrooms submerged in the wine. Leave for 30 minutes. Discard any tough stalks and slice the mushrooms if necessary (they are usually sold sliced in packets).

Melt the butter in a large saucepan. Add the chestnut mushrooms and cook for 5 minutes, stirring, then pour in the dried mushrooms and wine from soaking. Bring to the boil, reduce the heat and cook at a steady simmer for 15 minutes. Stir in the oyster mushrooms, cook for 2–3 minutes, then add the cream, seasoning and parsley. Heat gently, stirring, but do not boil or the sauce will curdle.

Add the drained pasta to the sauce, remove from the heat and mix well. Allow to stand, covered, for 2–3 minutes, then toss the pasta again and serve with grated parmesan cheese.

Cardamom Fish Sauce

Lemon and coriander pep up plain white fish in this delicious sauce. It is particularly good with spirals or small pieces of pasta, such as squares or cut-up spaghetti; saffron or turmeric pasta is ideal if you are making your own. For a first course, serve half quantities of sauce in small rings of saffron or turmeric noodles.

SERVES 4

25 g/1 oz butter

1 small onion, finely chopped

1 red pepper, seeded and diced

6 green cardamoms

1 bay leaf

grated rind of 1 lemon

25 g/1 oz plain flour

300 ml/½ pt fish stock

salt and freshly ground black pepper

675 g/1½ lb white fish fillet, skinned and cut into chunks

300 ml/½ pt single cream

2 tbsp chopped coriander leaves

Melt the butter in a saucepan. Add the onion, pepper, cardamoms, bay leaf and lemon rind. Press the cardamoms to split them slightly, then cook gently for 20 minutes, until the onion and pepper are well cooked. Stir often, so that the bay and spices give up their flavour and the onions do not brown.

Stir in the flour, then gradually pour in the stock, stirring all the time, and bring to the boil. Reduce the heat, if necessary, so that the sauce just simmers – it will be too thick at this stage. Add seasoning and the fish. Stir lightly, then cover the pan and cook gently for 20 minutes, or until the fish is cooked. Gently stir in the cream, then heat through without boiling. Taste for seasoning before serving sprinkled with the coriander.

Chicken and Tarragon Sauce

This is a simple sauce which goes well with any pasta. It may also be layered with lasagne, noodles or shapes in baked dishes. Turkey may be used instead of chicken.

SERVES 4

25–50 g/1–2 oz butter

1 small onion, finely chopped

1 bay leaf

100 g/4 oz button mushrooms, sliced

40 g/1½ oz plain flour

300 ml/½ pt chicken stock

150 ml/¼ pt milk

225–350 g/8–12 oz boneless, skinned, cooked chicken, diced

2 tbsp chopped tarragon

salt and freshly ground black pepper

150 ml/¼ pt single cream

Melt 25 g/1 oz butter in a saucepan. Add the onion and bay leaf and cook, stirring occasionally, for 15 minutes, or until the onion is softened slightly but not browned. Add the mushrooms and continue to cook for 10–15 minutes, until they give up their juice and this evaporates completely, leaving the reduced vegetables and the butter.

Stir in the flour, then gradually pour in the stock and bring to the boil, stirring all the time. Stir in the milk, bring back to the boil, then add the chicken and tarragon with seasoning to taste. Reduce the heat, cover the pan and simmer gently for 10 minutes. Stir in the cream and heat gently without boiling. If you like, beat in another 25 g/1 oz butter to enrich the sauce and make it rather special. Taste for seasoning before serving.

Duck and Orange Dressing

A rich dressing for narrow noodles or spaghetti, and a good way of making a couple of large duck breasts serve four. Make a salad of grated courgette and carrot as an accompaniment (see Cook's Tip).

SERVES 4

2 large boneless duck breasts, skinned and cut into fine strips
1 tbsp plain flour
salt and freshly ground black pepper
½ tsp ground mace
grated rind and juice of 1 orange
1 tbsp oil
1 onion, halved and thinly sliced
350 g/12 oz mushrooms, sliced
300 ml/½ pt dry red wine
4 tbsp redcurrant jelly

Place the duck meat in a bowl or polythene bag. Add the flour, plenty of seasoning, the mace and orange rind. Mix well, or close and shake the bag.

Heat the oil in a large frying pan. Add the duck and brown the strips all over, then add the onion and cook, stirring often, for about 15 minutes, or until the onion is softened slightly but not browned. Stir in the mushrooms and cook for 10 minutes or so, until they are well reduced. Pour in the orange juice and wine, then bring to the boil. Add the redcurrant jelly and boil for about 1 minute, stirring.

Taste for seasoning, then ladle the duck sauce over the pasta and serve at once.

COOK'S TIP

Carrot and Courgette Salad. Coarsely grate 3 carrots and 3 courgettes. Mix with a finely chopped spring onion and 4 shredded basil sprigs. Add 2 tbsp olive oil, a squeeze of orange juice and seasoning. Serve on a bed of iceberg lettuce.

Rich Meat Ragout

This is a good Bolognese-style sauce for ladling over pasta or layering with it.

SERVES 4

3 tbsp olive oil
1 large onion, chopped
2 celery sticks, finely diced
2 carrots, finely diced
1 green pepper, seeded and diced
2 garlic cloves, crushed
100 g/4 oz rindless smoked bacon, diced
2 tsp dried marjoram
1 thyme sprig
1 bay leaf
225 g/8 oz lean minced pork
225 g/8 oz lean minced braising steak
salt and freshly ground black pepper
1 tbsp plain flour
1 tbsp tomato purée
2 × 400 g/14 oz cans chopped tomatoes
300 ml/½ pt dry red wine
4 tbsp chopped parsley
freshly grated parmesan cheese, to serve

Heat the oil in a large, heavy-based saucepan. Add the onion, celery, carrots, green pepper, garlic, bacon, marjoram, thyme and bay leaf. Cook, stirring, until the onion is slightly softened and the bacon cooked – about 15 minutes.

Add the pork and steak and continue to cook, stirring, for 10 minutes to mix and lightly cook the meats. Stir in plenty of seasoning, the flour and tomato purée. Stir in the tomatoes and wine, then bring the sauce to the boil. Reduce the heat, cover, and simmer the sauce for 1½ hours. Stir the sauce occasionally during cooking.

At the end of cooking, taste and adjust the seasoning before mixing in the parsley and serving the sauce ladled over pasta. Serve with parmesan cheese.

Sausage Meatball Sauce

SERVES 4

450 g/1 lb pork sausagemeat

1 onion, finely chopped

1 garlic clove, crushed

¼ tsp chilli powder

1 tsp ground coriander

salt and freshly ground black pepper

1 tsp dried oregano

1 tsp chopped thyme

1 tbsp chopped sage

75 g/3 oz fresh breadcrumbs

1 egg

1 tbsp oil

1 green pepper, seeded and diced

225 g/8 oz button mushrooms

½ quantity Good Tomato Sauce

Place the sausagemeat in a bowl. Add the onion, garlic, chilli, coriander, seasoning, oregano, thyme, sage and breadcrumbs. Use a mixing spoon to break up the sausagemeat and mix in some of the other ingredients. When the sausagemeat is well broken up, add the egg. Then pound the ingredients together until thoroughly combined.

Wash your hands, then rinse them under cold water and keep them wet while you shape the meatballs to prevent the mixture sticking to them. Shape small, walnut-size meatballs.

Heat the oil in a large frying pan. Add the meatballs and brown them all over, using a spoon and fork to roll them around the pan. Add the green pepper and mushrooms and continue to cook for 10 minutes, or until the pepper is softened slightly. Pour in the tomato sauce and bring to the boil. Simmer for 20 minutes, turning the meatballs in the sauce occasionally. Serve piping hot.

Aubergine and Leek Topping

SERVES 4

2 large aubergines, trimmed and cubed

salt and freshly ground black pepper

4 tbsp olive oil

2 garlic cloves, crushed

1/4 tsp chilli powder

450 g/1 lb leeks, sliced

2 tbsp tahini

450 ml/3/4 pt stock (vegetable or chicken)

Place the aubergines in a colander and sprinkle them with salt, then leave them to stand over a bowl for 20 minutes. Rinse the aubergines well and leave to drain.

Heat half the olive oil in a large saucepan. Add some of the aubergine cubes and brown them on all sides. Use a slotted spoon to remove the cubes from the pan and set aside. Add more oil as necessary and cook the remaining cubes. Set aside. Add the garlic, chilli powder and leeks to the pan, then cook, stirring often, for 10 minutes, until the leeks are greatly reduced in volume.

Replace the aubergines and stir in the tahini, then pour in the stock and bring to the boil. Reduce the heat and cover the pan, then simmer for 15–20 minutes, until the aubergines and leeks are cooked through. Taste for seasoning before serving.

Broccoli and Baby Corn Dressing

SERVES 4

450 g/1 lb broccoli, cut into small florets

225 g/8 oz whole baby corn cobs

25 g/1 oz butter or 2 tbsp oil

1 onion, chopped

225 g/8 oz rindless bacon, diced

1 tbsp plain flour

salt and freshly ground black pepper

6 tbsp dry sherry

150 ml/¼ pt chicken or vegetable stock

freshly grated parmesan cheese, to serve

Place the broccoli in a steamer and cook over boiling water for 5 minutes. Add the baby corn cobs and cook for a further 5 minutes. Alternatively, cook the vegetables for the same time in the minimum of boiling water; they have a better flavour if they are steamed.

Melt the butter or heat the oil in a large saucepan. Add the onion and bacon, and cook, stirring often, until both are cooked. Stir in the flour and a little seasoning, then add the sherry and stock. Stir in the broccoli and corn. Bring to the boil, reduce the heat and cover the pan. Simmer for 5 minutes. Taste for seasoning.

Serve the vegetables and their sauce tossed into pasta. Offer parmesan cheese and extra ground pepper at the table.

Wonderful Mushroom Sauce

Look out for dried mushrooms in Italian and Eastern European delicatessens. This rich sauce, combining dried and fresh mushrooms, is delicious with plain noodles.

SERVES 4

2 whole dried mushrooms
150 ml/¼ pt boiling water
25 g/1 oz butter
1 tbsp olive oil
½ small onion, finely chopped
1 bay leaf
350 g/12 oz button mushrooms, sliced
100 ml/ 4 fl oz dry sherry
salt and freshly ground black pepper
350 g/12 oz oyster mushrooms
300 ml/½ pt single cream
3 tbsp chopped parsley
1 tbsp lemon juice

Place the dried mushrooms in a small basin and add the boiling water. Put a saucer on the mushrooms to keep them submerged and leave to soak for 15 minutes. Turn the mushrooms and the liquid into a small saucepan and simmer for 10 minutes, adding a little extra water if necessary. Drain, reserving the cooking liquor. Chop the mushrooms. Strain the liquor through a muslin-lined sieve or fine tea strainer to remove any grit.

Heat the butter and oil in a frying pan. Add the onion and bay leaf, then cook, stirring, for 5 minutes. Add the sliced mushrooms and continue to cook for 15–20 minutes. The mushrooms will give up their liquor and shrink: this stage is complete when all the liquid has evaporated, leaving the darkened mushrooms in the oil and butter, and it is important for a good flavour. Add the dried mushrooms and the strained liquid. Stir in the sherry and seasoning, then simmer for 5 minutes.

Add the oyster mushrooms and poach them in the sauce for 3 minutes, so that they are hot and lightly cooked. Stir in the cream, parsley and lemon juice. Heat gently without boiling. Taste for seasoning and serve ladled over fresh noodles.

Good Tomato Sauce

Good fresh pasta and a rich tomato sauce, topped with some freshly grated parmesan cheese, is a simple yet splendid meal, particularly if there is a really fresh, crisp green salad as an accompaniment. This sauce also has many uses in baked dishes or with stuffed pasta.

MAKES ABOUT 900 ML/1½ PT
SERVES 4–6

2 tbsp olive oil
1 large onion, chopped
1 carrot, chopped
1 celery stick, chopped
1 garlic clove, crushed
1 bay leaf
2 thyme sprigs
4 parsley sprigs
1 tbsp plain flour
2 tbsp tomato purée
900 g/2 lb ripe tomatoes, roughly chopped
1 tbsp sugar
150 ml/¼ pt dry red wine
salt and freshly ground black pepper
freshly grated parmesan cheese, to serve

Heat the oil in a large, heavy-based saucepan. Add the onion, carrot, celery, garlic, bay leaf, thyme and parsley. Cook, stirring, for 10 minutes, until the onion is softened slightly but not browned.

Stir in the flour and tomato purée. Then add the tomatoes and sugar and stir in the wine. Add some seasoning, bring to the boil and give the sauce a good stir. Reduce the heat, cover the pan and leave to simmer for 1 hour.

Remove the bay leaf and herb sprigs, then purée the sauce in a liquidizer and rub it through a sieve to remove the seeds. Reheat and taste for seasoning before serving. Ladle the sauce over pasta and top with parmesan cheese to taste.

Pesto

This is a wonderfully aromatic sauce based on basil. Grow a large pot of basil especially for the purpose of making pesto, or buy several cartons of the growing herb (if you plant the roots and shoots from the base of such cartons they will grow into large, healthy plants). Although pesto is traditionally made by pounding all the ingredients using a pestle and mortar, a food processor or liquidizer is more or less essential for the busy cook. If you do not have either, then work in far smaller quantities than those given below.

MAKES ABOUT 600 ML/1 PT

175 g/6 oz fresh parmesan cheese, rind removed
100 g/4 oz pine kernels
4 garlic cloves
50 g/2 oz basil sprigs (soft stems and leaves only, discard tough stalks before weighing)
350–450 ml/12–15 fl oz good-quality virgin olive oil
salt and freshly ground black pepper

Break the parmesan into small pieces and place in the food processor with the pine kernels and garlic. Process the mixture until the parmesan is finely crumbled. Add the basil and continue processing until the herb is chopped and the mixture begins to clump together into a coarse, bright green paste.

Add a little of the olive oil and process the mixture until it is incorporated, then gradually trickle in the remaining olive oil. Add enough to make a thin, pouring paste. Add seasoning to taste.

If using a liquidizer, process the mixture in batches. The oil does not form a mayonnaise-like liaison: it will separate on standing and the paste has to be stirred again. Mix all the batches together at the end so that the ingredients are combined in the correct proportions.

Transfer the pesto to a clean screw-top jar and store it in the refrigerator. The oil acts as a preservative and the pesto will keep for several months if stored in an airtight container in the refrigerator. Stir it well before using.

Top individual portions of pasta with a couple of spoons of pesto, then toss together and eat at once – delicious!

COOK'S TIP

If you are making a large batch of pesto for storing, sterilize the jars and their lids in a proprietary brand of sterilizing solution (from chemists; used for babies' bottles or for home brewing), then rinse them with boiling water and allow to dry by draining. Leave the jars upside down until you fill them with pesto.

LEFT
Tomatoes and grapes on a courtyard table . . . wonderful ingredients for fresh pasta recipes.

Béchamel Sauce

Well-cooked, good-quality pasta makes a delicious meal with the minimum of additions: in the Italian kitchen that means olive oil and garlic or butter with parmesan; to the traditional British cook a good milk-based sauce is ideal. Béchamel is a basic milk sauce which is lightly flavoured with bay and mace: it is used in a variety of pasta dishes, notably as the topping for baked lasagne.

MAKES ABOUT 600 ML/1 PT

1 thick onion slice
1 bay leaf
1 mace blade
2 parsley sprigs
600 ml/1 pt milk
40 g/1½ oz butter
40 g/1½ oz plain flour
salt and freshly ground white or black pepper

Place the onion, bay leaf, mace and parsley in a saucepan. Add the milk and heat slowly until just boiling. Remove from the heat, cover and leave for 45 minutes.

Strain the milk into a jug or basin. Wash the saucepan, then melt the butter and stir in the flour. Slowly pour in the milk, stirring all the time. Continue stirring until the sauce boils, then reduce the heat, if necessary, so that it just simmers. Cook for 3 minutes, stirring occasionally. Add seasoning to taste.

If the sauce is not used straight away, lay a piece of dampened greaseproof paper directly on its surface to prevent a skin forming.

Variations

Any one of the following may be mixed with freshly cooked pasta and served as a light meal. A gratin topping may be added by sprinkling the sauced pasta with 25 g/1 oz fresh breadcrumbs mixed with 2 tbsp freshly grated parmesan cheese and browning under the grill.

Cheese Sauce Stir in 100 g/4 oz grated mature Cheddar cheese and 4 tbsp freshly grated parmesan cheese after the sauce has simmered.

Egg Sauce Hard-boil and roughly chop 6 eggs, then mix them into the cooked sauce. Add 1 tbsp chopped tarragon or parsley, or 2 tbsp chopped dill, if liked.

Mushroom Sauce Add 225 g/8 oz sliced button mushrooms before the final simmering.

Onion Sauce Finely chop 2 large onions. Cook them in the butter for about 20 minutes, stirring often, until they are softened. Do not allow the onions to brown but do make sure that they are well cooked, otherwise the sauce will be inferior. Stir in the flour and continue as above.

Tuna Sauce Drain a 200 g/7 oz can of tuna. Flake the fish and add it to the sauce before the final simmering. Add 2 tbsp chopped parsley and 1 tbsp capers, chopped.

Tuna may be added to mushroom sauce, or an onion sauce may be prepared, then both mushrooms and tuna added. The oil from the can may be used instead of butter; brine may be added to the sauce with milk.

White Wine Sauce

MAKES 600 ML/1 PT

50 g/2 oz butter

1 small onion, finely chopped

1 bay leaf

2 parsley sprigs with long stalks

50 g/2 oz button mushrooms, thinly sliced

40 g/1½ oz plain flour

300 ml/½ pt dry white wine

*150 ml/¼ pt stock (chicken, vegetable or fish,
depending on the dish)*

salt and freshly ground white or black pepper

300 ml/½ pt single cream

Melt the butter in a saucepan. Add the onion, bay leaf and parsley, then cook, stirring often, for 15 minutes, until the onion is softened slightly but not browned. Stir in the mushrooms, then stir in the flour. Gradually stir in the white wine and stock, then bring to the boil. The sauce will be too thick at this stage. Cover the pan tightly and allow the sauce to cook very gently for 15 minutes.

Add seasoning and beat the sauce well. Remove the bay leaf and parsley sprigs. Stir in the cream and heat gently without boiling.

BELOW
*Vines growing at Monte
Reggiano, Italy.*

Chicken and Ham Lasagne

This is easy and delicious! Turkey may be used instead of chicken – a great way of using up the Christmas roast. Add any leftover stuffing to the sauce too.

SERVES 6–8

350 g/12 oz spinach-flavoured pasta dough or fresh lasagne verdi

2 quantities Béchamel Sauce

225 g/8 oz skinned, boneless cooked chicken, diced

225 g/8 oz lean cooked ham, diced

100 g/4 oz button mushrooms, chopped

6 spring onions, chopped

2 tbsp chopped parsley

1 tbsp chopped sage

salt and freshly ground black pepper

75 g/3 oz Caerphilly, Lancashire or Wensleydale cheese, finely crumbled

paprika

25 g/1 oz fresh white breadcrumbs

Prepare and cook the lasagne as for Classic Lasagne al Forno. Butter a 30–38 × 20 cm/12–15 × 8 in ovenproof dish and set the oven at 180°C/350°F/Gas 4.

Set aside a third of the béchamel sauce. Mix the chicken, ham, mushrooms, spring onions, parsley and sage with the rest of the sauce. Taste for seasoning, then layer this sauce in the dish with the lasagne, ending with a layer of lasagne on top. Stir the cheese into the reserved sauce (it doesn't matter if the sauce is too cool for it to melt), then spread it over the top of the pasta. Sprinkle with a little paprika and top with the breadcrumbs.

Bake for 40–50 minutes, until the topping is crisp and golden and the lasagne layers are bubbling hot.

COOK'S TIP

A mixture of crushed crisps and a few finely chopped salted peanuts added to the breadcrumbs makes a good topping.

Classic Lasagne Al Forno

SERVES 6–8

350 g/12 oz pasta dough or fresh lasagne

salt and freshly ground black pepper

butter for greasing

1 quantity Rich Meat Ragout

1½ quantities Béchamel Sauce

25 g/1 oz freshly grated parmesan cheese

Cut the rolled-out pasta into large squares (about 12.5 cm/5 in) or oblong sheets. Lower the pieces of pasta one at a time into a large saucepan of boiling salted water. Bring back to the boil and cook for 3 minutes. Drain and rinse under cold water. Lay the pasta on double-thick sheets of absorbent kitchen paper.

Set the oven at 180°C/350°F/Gas 4. Butter a large oblong ovenproof dish (about 30–38 × 20 cm/12–15 × 8 in). Ladle a little of the ragout into the dish and spread it out. Dot with a little of the béchamel sauce, then add a layer of pasta. Continue layering the meat, a little béchamel and pasta, ending with pasta. Do not include much béchamel between the layers as you need most of it to cover the top of the lasagne. Sprinkle the parmesan over the top and bake the lasagne for 45–50 minutes, until golden brown and bubbling hot.

Tagliatelle Turkey Bake

SERVES 4–6

2 tbsp olive oil
1 onion, chopped
1 garlic clove, crushed
1 green pepper, seeded and diced
1 tsp dried marjoram
350 g/12 oz skinned, boneless cooked turkey, diced
100 g/4 oz mushrooms, thinly sliced
400 g/14 oz can chopped tomatoes
3 tbsp chopped parsley
salt and freshly ground black pepper
450 g/1 lb tagliatelle, cooked
4 fresh basil sprigs
600 ml/1 pint Béchamel Sauce (page 58)
100 g/4 oz mozzarella cheese, diced
2 tbsp freshly grated parmesan cheese

Set the oven at 200°C/400°F/Gas 6. Heat the oil in a large saucepan. Add the onion, garlic, green pepper and marjoram. Cook, stirring often, for 15–20 minutes, until the onion is softened. Stir in the turkey, mushrooms, tomatoes, parsley and seasoning. Remove from the heat and mix in the tagliatelle. Turn the mixture into an ovenproof dish and press the top down with the back of a metal spoon so the noodles are fairly flat.

Use scissors to shred the basil and soft stalks into the béchamel sauce. Taste for seasoning, then pour the sauce evenly over the pasta mixture. Mix the mozzarella and parmesan, then sprinkle this over the sauce. Bake for 40–45 minutes, until the topping is browned.

Tuna Triangles

SERVES 6–8

200 g/7 oz can tuna, drained

2 tbsp finely chopped spring onion

1 garlic clove, crushed

50 g/2 oz fresh white breadcrumbs

grated rind of ½ lemon

4 tbsp freshly grated parmesan cheese

salt and freshly ground black pepper

about 3 tbsp milk

⅔ quantity pasta dough

1 egg, beaten

*Good Tomato Sauce,
White Wine Sauce,
Cheese Sauce or Mushroom Sauce*

freshly grated parmesan cheese, to serve

Mash the tuna, then mix in the spring onion, garlic and breadcrumbs. Add the lemon rind, parmesan cheese and seasoning to taste. Mix in just enough milk to bind the mixture.

Roll out half the pasta dough into a 32 cm/ 12½ in square. Cut it into 5 × 6 cm/2½ in strips, then cut these across into squares. Brush a square of dough with a little egg. Place a little tuna mixture on the middle of the dough, then fold it in half in a triangular shape. Pinch the edges together well to seal in the filling. Repeat with the remainder of the rolled dough, then do the same with the second half.

Bring a large saucepan of salted water to the boil. Add the triangles and bring the water back to the boil. Do not let the water boil too rapidly or the pasta may burst: keep it just boiling steadily. Cook for 4–5 minutes, then drain well.

Serve the triangles with any one of the sauces listed and offer parmesan cheese at the table.

Savoury Sardine Cannelloni

An inexpensive dish for a mid-week meal. The sardine and cheese mixture is also good for filling ravioli or tortellini.

SERVES 4

⅓ quantity pasta dough

2 × 120 g/4 oz cans sardines in oil

1 onion, chopped

1 garlic clove, crushed

75 g/3 oz fresh white breadcrumbs

100 g/4 oz mushrooms, chopped

100 g/4 oz curd cheese

100 g/4 oz Cheddar cheese, grated

grated rind and juice of 1 lemon

salt and freshly ground black pepper

butter for greasing

1 quantity Good Tomato Sauce

Roll out the pasta into a thin 40 cm/16 in square. Cut it into 4 × 10 cm/4 in wide strips, then cut the strips across to make 16 squares. Bring a large pan of salted water to the boil and cook the pieces of pasta, a few at a time if necessary, for 3 minutes. Drain and rinse under cold water, then lay out on double-thick absorbent kitchen paper.

Pour the oil from the sardines into a small saucepan. Add the onion and garlic, then cook, stirring often, for 10 minutes. Remove from the heat. Mash the sardines and add them to the onion and garlic. Mix in the breadcrumbs, mushrooms, curd cheese, three-quarters of the Cheddar cheese, the lemon rind and juice, and seasoning to taste.

Set the oven at 200°C/400°F/Gas 6. Butter an ovenproof dish. Place some of the sardine mixture on a piece of pasta, then roll it up into a neat tube and place in the dish with the end of the roll underneath. Repeat with the remaining pasta and filling. Ladle the tomato sauce over the cannelloni, then sprinkle with the remaining cheese. Bake for 25–30 minutes, until the cheese has melted and browned. Serve at once.

Chicken Tortellini

SERVES 6–8

225 g/8 oz skinned, boneless cooked chicken, minced
25 g/1 oz fresh white breadcrumbs
2 tbsp very finely chopped onion
1 tbsp chopped sage
2 tbsp chopped parsley
4 tbsp single cream or milk
salt and freshly ground black pepper
2/3 quantity pasta dough
1 egg, beaten
White Wine Sauce or *Good Tomato Sauce*
freshly grated parmesan cheese, to serve

Mix the chicken, breadcrumbs, onion, sage, parsley and cream or milk. Add seasoning and pound the mixture with the spoon to ensure all the ingredients are thoroughly combined.

Cut the pasta dough in half. Roll out one piece into a 30 cm/12 in square – it is a good idea to roll the dough nominally larger, then trim it neatly. Cut the dough into 6 × 5 cm/2 in strips, then cut across these to make 5 cm/2 in squares. Brush a square of dough with a little egg, then place a little of the chicken filling in the middle of it. Seal two opposite corners together to make a triangular shape. Wrap the long side of the triangle around your fingertip and pinch the corners together to make a mitre shape (or bishop's hat shape). Continue filling and sealing the tortellini, then roll out the second portion of dough and repeat the process. Do not overfill the tortellini or they will burst during cooking.

Bring a large saucepan of salted water to the boil. Add the tortellini and bring the water back to the boil. Do not boil the pasta too rapidly or they will split. Cook for 5 minutes, then drain well. Serve the tortellini with White Wine Sauce or Good Tomato Sauce and offer parmesan cheese at the table.

Alternative Serving Ideas
▌ Toss the tortellini in hot melted butter and parmesan cheese.
▌ Serve with Béchamel Sauce.
▌ Serve with Pesto.
▌ Serve the tortellini in soup, such as consommé or chicken broth.

Walnut Cheese Ravioli

SERVES 6

2 tbsp olive oil

1 small onion, finely chopped

1 garlic clove, crushed

100 g/4 oz walnuts, finely chopped

100 g/4 oz ricotta cheese

75 g/3 oz gruyère cheese

2 tbsp freshly grated parmesan cheese

6 basil sprigs, finely shredded

50 g/2 oz fresh white breadcrumbs

salt and freshly ground black pepper

⅔ quantity pasta dough

1 egg, beaten

White Wine Sauce or hot melted butter to serve

Heat the oil in a small saucepan. Add the onion and garlic and cook for 15 minutes, until the onion is softened but not browned. Remove from the heat, then stir in the walnuts, ricotta, gruyère, parmesan cheese, basil and breadcrumbs. Add seasoning to taste and mix the ingredients thoroughly.

Make the ravioli as for the Beef Ravioli with Tomato Sauce, making sure the mixture is well sealed in the packets. Cook the ravioli for 5 minutes in water which is just boiling, as the cheese filling does not take as long to cook through as the raw beef filling. Drain and serve with Wine Sauce or simply with butter and pepper.

Spinach and Ricotta Tortellini

SERVES 6–8

175 g/6 oz fresh spinach, trimmed and cooked

100 g/4 oz ricotta cheese

4 tbsp freshly grated parmesan cheese

25 g/1 oz fresh white breadcrumbs

pinch of dried thyme

1 tsp dried marjoram

a little freshly grated nutmeg

salt and freshly ground black pepper

²/₃ quantity pasta dough

1 egg, beaten

Make sure the spinach is thoroughly drained, then chop it finely. Mix it with the ricotta, parmesan, breadcrumbs and herbs. Add a little nutmeg and seasoning to taste.

Use the dough and beaten egg to make and fill the tortellini, following the instructions for Chicken Tortellini. Cook and serve the tortellini in the same way.

Smoked Salmon and Pasta Cocktails

This turns a comparatively small quantity of smoked salmon into an attractive starter.

SERVES 4

100 g/4 oz fresh pasta spirals

4 tbsp mayonnaise

4 tbsp soured cream

2 tbsp snipped chives

salt and freshly ground black pepper

4 endive or frisée leaves, roughly shredded

175 g/6 oz smoked salmon, shredded

2 tbsp chopped dill

grated rind of ¹/₂ lemon

dill sprigs, to garnish

4 lemon wedges, to serve

Cook the pasta in boiling salted water for 3 minutes. Drain and cool. Mix the mayonnaise, soured cream and chives with the pasta. Add seasoning to taste.

Arrange the endive or frisée in four glass dishes then divide the pasta between the dishes. Mix the smoked salmon with the dill and lemon rind, then arrange the shreds on top of the pasta. Garnish with dill sprigs. Serve lemon wedges with the cocktails so that their juice may be sprinkled over the smoked salmon.

Crab and Courgette Salad

SERVES 4

225 g/8 oz fresh pasta shapes

225 g/8 oz small, young courgettes

6 spring onions, chopped

6 basil sprigs

salt and freshly ground black pepper

2 tbsp lemon juice

2 tbsp olive oil

175 g/6 oz crab meat

4 eggs, hard-boiled

4 tbsp chopped parsley

Cook the pasta in boiling salted water for 3 minutes. Drain well and place in a bowl. Trim and coarsely grate the courgettes, then add them to the pasta with the spring onions. Use scissors to shred the basil and soft stalk ends into the salad. Sprinkle in seasoning to taste and mix in the lemon juice. Add the olive oil and mix well. Arrange the mixture in a serving dish, leaving a hollow in the middle.

Flake the crab meat. Chop the eggs and mix them with the crab. Fork in the parsley and seasoning to taste, then spoon the mixture in the middle of the pasta. Serve at once; if the salad is allowed to stand the pasta and courgettes become watery.

Ham and Avocado Salad

SERVES 4

350 g/12 oz fresh pasta shapes

2 tbsp cider vinegar

1 tsp prepared wholegrain mustard

½ tsp caster sugar

salt and freshly ground black pepper

6 tbsp olive oil

450 g/1 lb lean cooked ham (in one piece), cubed

2 avocados

4 tbsp snipped chives

50 g/2 oz walnuts, chopped

1 lettuce heart or ½ iceberg lettuce, shredded (optional)

Cook the pasta in boiling salted water for 3 minutes, then drain well. Meanwhile, mix the cider vinegar, mustard, caster sugar and seasoning in a basin. Whisk the mixture until the sugar and salt have dissolved. Gradually whisk in the oil. Turn the hot pasta into a dish and pour the dressing over it, then mix well.

Allow the pasta to cool slightly before mixing in the ham. Just before serving the salad, halve the avocados, remove their stones and quarter the halves lengthways. Remove the peel, then cut the flesh into chunks and mix them with the pasta. Mix in the chives and walnuts.

Arrange the salad on a base of shredded lettuce, if liked, and serve promptly. If the salad is allowed to stand, the avocado will discolour.

Spaghetti and Salami Salad

SERVES 4

350 g/12 oz fresh spaghetti

4 tbsp pine kernels

175 g/6 oz salami, cut in strips

50 g/2 oz black olives, pitted and sliced

425 g/15 oz can artichoke hearts, drained

2 tbsp cider vinegar

salt and freshly ground black pepper

½ tsp caster sugar

6 tbsp olive oil

4 tbsp chopped parsley

Cut the spaghetti into 5 cm/2 in lengths, then cook it in boiling salted water for 3 minutes. Drain the pasta well in a fine sieve before tipping it into a bowl; leave to cool.

Roast the pine kernels in a small, dry, heavy-bottomed saucepan until they are lightly browned, then tip them over the pasta. Add the salami, olives and artichoke hearts. Mix the cider vinegar, seasoning and caster sugar in a screw-top jar. Shake well until the sugar dissolves, then add the olive oil and shake again.

Pour the dressing over the salad and mix well. Toss the parsley in after the dressing, immediately before serving the salad.

Frankfurter Supper

SERVES 4

225 g/8 oz fresh pasta shapes or small pasta squares

1/2 small onion, chopped

225 g/8 oz white cabbage, shredded

2 carrots, coarsely grated

150 ml/1/4 pt mayonnaise

8 frankfurters, sliced

salt and freshly ground black pepper

4 tbsp chopped roasted peanuts

Cook the pasta in boiling salted water for 3 minutes, then drain it and allow to cool. Mix the onion, cabbage, carrots and mayonnaise. Toss the pasta and frankfurters with the cabbage mixture and seasoning. Divide between four serving bowls. Sprinkle with peanuts and serve at once, offering plenty of warmed crusty bread with the salad.

Mixed Pasta Salad

A good one for all those parties and picnics!

SERVES 4

225 g/8 oz pasta shapes

100 g/4 oz frozen sweetcorn

100 g/4 oz frozen peas

1 carrot, diced

4 celery sticks, diced

1 green pepper, seeded and diced

6 spring onions, chopped

2 tbsp chopped parsley

250 ml/8 fl oz mayonnaise

3 tbsp single cream

225 g/8 oz garlic sausage, roughly chopped

salt and freshly ground black pepper

Cook the pasta in boiling salted water for 3 minutes, drain well, then turn the pasta into a bowl. Place the sweetcorn, peas and carrot in a saucepan and add water to cover. Bring to the boil, add the celery and bring back to the boil, then cook for 5 minutes. Drain the vegetables and add them to the pasta. Allow to cool.

Mix in the green pepper, spring onions and parsley. Thin the mayonnaise with the cream, then toss this dressing into the salad. Lastly, lightly mix in the garlic sausage and taste for seasoning.

Won Ton Soup

SERVES 4

225 g/8 oz minced pork

4 spring onions, finely chopped

2 button mushrooms, finely chopped

2 tbsp soy sauce

1 tsp sesame oil

½ quantity won ton dough

1 egg, beaten

1 tbsp oil

1 boneless chicken breast, skinned and diced

2 leeks, sliced

900 ml/1½ pt good chicken stock

4 tbsp dry sherry

salt and freshly ground black pepper

Mix the pork, spring onions, mushrooms, soy sauce and sesame oil. Roll out the dough into a 37.5 cm/ 15 in square, dusting the surface with cornflour as necessary. The dough should be very thin. Cut the dough into 7.5 cm/3 in strips, then across into squares. Cover the dough with cling film.

To fill the won tons, take a square of dough and roll it again so that it is paper thin. Shape a little meat into a ball and place it in the middle of the dough square. Brush the meat with egg, then fold the dough around it and pinch it together to seal in the meat. Leave the corners of the dough hanging free. Fill all the won tons in the same way and place them on a platter or board dusted with cornflour.

For the soup, heat the oil in a saucepan. Add the chicken and leeks, and cook, stirring often, for 20 minutes, until the leek is softened and the chicken is just cooked. Pour in the stock and bring to the boil. Cover and simmer for 20 minutes. Stir in the sherry and seasoning to taste. Add the won tons to the soup, bring back to the boil and reduce the heat slightly so that it does not boil fiercely. Cook for 5 minutes. Test a won ton to make sure the filling is cooked, then ladle the soup and won tons into bowls. Serve at once.

Crispy Won Tons

These won tons are made in the same way as the ones which are cooked in soup; however, they are deep fried until crisp and served with a sweet and sour sauce. Offer them as a first course for a Chinese meal or serve them with plain boiled rice and a dish of stir-fried vegetables to make a delicious main course.

SERVES 4

won tons as for Won Ton Soup
oil for deep frying

For the sauce

2 tbsp oil
1 tsp sesame oil
1 onion, halved and thinly sliced
1 green pepper, halved, seeded and thinly sliced
1 carrot, cut into fine 2.5 cm/1 in strips
4 tbsp tomato ketchup
4 tbsp soy sauce
1 tbsp sugar
2 tbsp cider vinegar
150 ml/¼ pt dry sherry
1 tsp cornflour
2 canned pineapple rings, cut in small pieces

Make the won tons as for the soup. Set them aside until the sauce is ready. Heat the oil and sesame oil in a saucepan. Add the onion, green pepper and carrot and cook for 5 minutes. Stir in the tomato ketchup, soy sauce, sugar, cider vinegar and sherry. Bring to the boil, reduce the heat and simmer for 3 minutes. Meanwhile, blend the cornflour with 2 tbsp cold water, then stir it into the sauce and bring to the boil, stirring all the time. Simmer for 2 minutes, then add the pineapple and set aside over low heat.

Heat the oil for deep frying to 190°C/375°F. Deep fry the won tons a few at a time, until they are crisp and golden. Drain them on absorbent kitchen paper. Place the won tons on a large flat dish or platter and spoon the sauce over them. Serve and eat at once.

LEFT
Boats on the Li River in southern China.

Prawn and Pork Dim Sum

MAKES 25

225 g/8 oz peeled cooked prawns, minced

100 g/4 oz minced pork

2 spring onions, finely chopped

1 tsp sesame oil

1 garlic clove, crushed

2 tsp soy sauce

½ quantity won ton dough

1 egg, beaten

soy sauce, to serve

The prawns may be finely chopped in the food processor or liquidizer. Mix them with the pork, spring onions, sesame oil, garlic and soy sauce. Pound the mixture well so that all the ingredients bind together. Wet your hands and shape the mixture into 25 small balls.

Roll out the won ton dough into a 31 cm/12.5 in square. Dust the surface with cornflour as necessary to prevent the dough from sticking. Cut the dough into 5 × 6 cm/2½ in strips, then cut them across into squares. Brush a square of dough with a little beaten egg. Hold the dough on the palm of your hand and place a prawn ball on it. Flatten the prawn ball slightly and bring the dough up and around it, leaving the top of the mixture uncovered. Brush the dough with a little extra egg, if necessary, so that the folds cling to the side of the mixture. Shape the remaining dim sum in the same way – they should have flattened bases and the dough should be wrinkled around their sides.

Place the dim sum on a greased shallow dish which will fit in a steamer, then steam them over rapidly boiling water for 15 minutes, or until the prawn mixture is cooked. While the dim sum are cooking, prepare small dishes of soy sauce. Serve the dim sum freshly cooked: they may be dipped into the soy sauce before eating.

Mushroom Dim Sum

These are an excellent vegetarian alternative to the usual dim sum filled with pork or prawns.

MAKES ABOUT 50 – SERVES 4

4 large Chinese dried mushrooms
4 Chinese cabbage leaves
½ × 200 g/7 oz can water chestnuts, drained and chopped
4 spring onions, chopped
100 g/4 oz button mushrooms, finely chopped
1 garlic clove, crushed
2 tbsp cornflour
salt
1 egg, beaten
1 quantity won ton dough

For the sauce

1 tbsp oil
1 tsp sesame oil
2 spring onions, chopped
15 g/½ oz fresh root ginger, peeled and finely shredded
1 celery stick, cut into fine 2.5 cm/1 in strips
1 carrot, cut into fine 2.5 cm/1 in strips
sherry (see method)
2 tsp cornflour
2 tbsp soy sauce

Place the mushrooms in a mug or very small basin. Add just enough boiling water to cover them, then put a small saucer over them and weight it down to keep the mushrooms submerged. Leave to stand for 20 minutes. Blanch the Chinese cabbage leaves in boiling water for 30 seconds, so they are just limp. Drain and squeeze all the water from them, then chop them finely.

Drain the mushrooms, reserving the soaking liquid in a measuring jug and squeezing the water from the mushrooms. Discard any woody stalks, then chop the mushroom caps and mix them with the Chinese leaves. Add the water chestnuts, spring onions, button mushrooms and garlic. Stir in the cornflour and salt to taste. Add a little beaten egg to bind the mixture, so that it clumps easily.

Prepare a large platter for the dim sum and dust it with cornflour. Cut the won ton dough in half. Roll out one portion into a 37.5 cm/15 in square, keeping the surface lightly dusted with cornflour. Cut the dough into 5 × 7.5 cm/3 in strips, then across into squares. Brush a square of dough with beaten egg, then place a little of the mushroom mixture on it. Gather the dough up around the filling to make a small bundle. Press the dough together at the top to seal in the filling. Fill all the squares of dough in the same way, then roll out the second half and repeat the process. Place the dim sum on the floured platter and cover loosely with cling film while you fill the remainder.

For the sauce, heat the oil and sesame oil together in a small saucepan. Add the spring onions, ginger, celery and carrot. Stir-fry for 2 minutes. Measure the soaking liquid from the mushrooms and add enough sherry to make it up to 300 ml/½ pt. Blend the cornflour to a smooth, thin paste with a little of the liquid, then stir in the rest of the liquid. Pour this into the pan, add the soy sauce and bring to the boil, stirring. Reduce the heat and taste for seasoning. Leave to simmer very gently.

Bring a large saucepan of salted water to the boil. Add the dim sum, bring back to the boil and cook for 5 minutes. Do not boil the water rapidly. Drain well and place in a warmed serving dish. Ladle the sauce over the dim sum and serve.

COOK'S TIP

The dim sum cook very well by steaming but this does require a lot of steamer space. Several layers of bamboo steamer, placed on a wok, are ideal and the dim sum should be placed in greased shallow dishes or on plates. If the plates are not greased the dim sum will stick.

Semolina Cheese Gnocchi

Gnocchi, small Italian dumplings, are usually grouped as close relatives of pasta. There are various ways of making gnocchi and using semolina is one common method.

SERVES 4

900 ml/1½ pt milk
1 bay leaf
1 mace blade
225 g/8 oz semolina
100 g/4 oz parmesan cheese, freshly grated
salt and freshly ground black pepper
2 eggs
50 g/2 oz lightly salted butter
shredded basil or chopped parsley, to serve

Pour the milk into a large pan and add the bay leaf and mace. Bring the milk slowly to the boil, then cover and remove from the heat. Allow the bay and mace to infuse for 45–60 minutes. Bring the milk back to just below boiling point, remove the bay and mace, then stir in the semolina. Cook, stirring all the time, until the mixture boils and thickens. It will become very stiff, so you have to work quite hard at stirring. This takes about 12–15 minutes.

Off the heat, beat in the parmesan cheese and seasoning. Allow the mixture to cool slightly before beating in the eggs. Grease a baking tin (a tray or roasting tin will do) and spread the gnocchi mixture out so that it is about 1 cm/½ in thick. Cover, leave until completely cold, then chill for at least a couple of hours.

Set the oven at 200°C/400°F/Gas 6. Use a little of the butter to grease an ovenproof dish. Cut the gnocchi into squares and arrange them in the dish. Melt the remaining butter and trickle it over the gnocchi, then bake for 20 minutes, until golden brown and crisp on top. Sprinkle with basil or parsley and serve at once.

Potato Gnocchi

These may be served with Meat Ragout, Good Tomato Sauce, Pesto or Cheese Sauce. If you are looking for a simple, satisfying supper, then simply toss them with butter, freshly ground black pepper and lots of grated cheese – parmesan or another type of your choice.

SERVES 4

450 g/1 lb potatoes
25 g/1 oz butter
175 g/6 oz strong plain flour
1 tsp salt
1 egg
a little freshly grated nutmeg

Boil the potatoes in their skins until tender, about 20–30 minutes, depending on size. Drain and peel the potatoes under cold running water. Then mash them and rub the mashed potato through a fine sieve into a bowl.

Add the butter to the potato and mix well. Mix in the flour and salt, then add the egg and a little nutmeg. Mix the ingredients with a spoon at first, then use your hand to bring them together into a dough. Knead lightly until smooth.

Bring a large pan of salted water to the boil. Shape a lump of the dough into a thick sausage, then cut off small pieces, about 2.5 cm/1 in long, and indent each piece, either with your finger or with a fork. Drop the gnocchi into the boiling water, bring back to the boil and cook for 4–5 minutes. The water must not boil too rapidly and the cooked gnocchi should be firm and tender – do not overcook them or they will become soggy and watery. Use a slotted spoon to remove the gnocchi from the pan if you are cooking them in batches. Drain well and serve at once with melted butter, pepper and parmesan.

Rum and Raisin Shapes

SERVES 6

50 g/2 oz raisins, chopped

25 g/1 oz candied peel, finely chopped

100 g/4 oz ground almonds

2 tbsp icing sugar

8 tbsp rum

⅔ quantity pasta dough

1 egg, beaten

175 g/6 oz crab apple jelly

4 tbsp unsweetened apple juice

2 tbsp finely chopped candied orange peel,
to decorate

Greek-style yogurt or cream, to serve

Mix the raisins, candied peel, almonds and icing sugar. Stir in enough of the rum to bind the ingredients together; the rest of the rum is required for the glaze.

Roll out, cut and fill the pasta as for Spiced Apricot Rounds. When all the pasta is filled, cook in boiling water for 5 minutes and drain well. To make the glaze, gently heat the crab apple jelly with the apple juice until the jelly melts. Bring to the boil, then remove from the heat and stir in the remaining rum.

Serve the pasta coated with the apple glaze. Sprinkle with the chopped candied orange peel and offer Greek-style yogurt or cream with the pasta.

Plum and Blackberry Compote

A good autumnal sauce for serving with plain home-made pasta. Remember that dessert pasta looks more attractive if it is stamped out in pretty shapes using aspic cutters.

SERVES 6

100 g/4 oz sugar
grated rind and juice of 1 orange
150 ml/¼ pt dry cider
1 cinnamon stick
2 cloves
450 g/1 lb plums, halved and stoned
450 g/1 lb blackberries

Place the sugar, orange rind and juice, cider, cinnamon and cloves in a large saucepan. Heat gently, stirring, until the sugar melts. Allow the syrup to infuse over very low heat for 15 minutes, then bring it to simmering point and add the plums.

Poach the plums gently for 3 minutes, then add the blackberries and cook for 2 minutes. (Do not overcook the fruit until it becomes soft; the cooking time for the plums varies according to their texture.) Ladle this fruit sauce over the pasta, removing the spices as you do so.

Chocolate Bows with White Chocolate Sauce

The unusual combination of the pasta texture and sweet flavour may not be to everyone's liking but chocolate fans will approve.

SERVES 4

⅓ quantity pasta dough
2 tbsp cocoa powder
3 tbsp icing sugar
1 tbsp walnut oil
1 tsp natural vanilla essence
225 g/8 oz white chocolate
3 tbsp golden syrup
25 g/1 oz unsalted butter
50 g/2 oz walnuts, chopped

Make the pasta dough, adding the cocoa and icing sugar to the flour before mixing in the egg and using 1 tbsp walnut oil and the vanilla essence instead of the olive oil. Roll out the dough into a 30 cm/12 in square.

Cut the dough into 3 cm/1½ in strips, then cut them across into 3 cm/1½ in squares. Pinch the opposite corners of a square of dough together, pleating the dough in the middle of the square and pressing it firmly, to make a small bow with pointed ends. Set the bow aside on a surface dusted with icing sugar. Do not cover the bows.

Before cooking the bows, prepare the white chocolate sauce. Break the chocolate into squares and place in a heatproof basin. Add the golden syrup and butter, then stand the bowl over a small saucepan of barely simmering water. Stir until the chocolate melts and the sauce is smooth. Turn the heat off and set the pan and bowl aside.

Cook the bows in just-boiling water for 3 minutes. Meanwhile, pour some chocolate sauce on warmed plates. Drain the bows, then arrange them on the sauce. Sprinkle with nuts and serve at once.